DAVE DUT...

COMPLETELY
LANKY

AURORA
Publishing

© Aurora Enterprises Ltd.

Published by Aurora Publishing,
Unit 18, Bolholt Industrial Park,
Walshaw Road,
Bury BL8 1PY.
Tel: 0161 705 2202

ISBN No 1 872226 61 2

COMPLETELY LANKY is a reprinted version of:
Lanky Panky by Dave Dutton &
Lanky Spoken Here by Dave Dutton

Edited by Cliff Hayes

Illustrations by:
Tony Griffiths — lives in Halewood, near Liverpool.
Tony, married with 3 children, works for Granada TV.

Ernest Andrew — otherwise known to the police as
'The Droylsden Dauber'.

Reprinted 1999

Printed & bound by MFP Design & Print,
Longford Trading Estate, Thomas Street,
Stretford, Manchester M32 0JT.
Tel: 0161 864 4540

INTRODUCTION

When I wrote 'Lanky Spoken Here' in 1978, my original title (grammatically correct from a Lanky point of view) was 'Lanky *Spokken* Here'. The Southern publisher, thinking it to be a spelling mistake, dropped a letter K — hence the title.

I am glad to say that the present book you hold in your hands (or teeth if you're that way inclined) is being published by Northerners. When the editor, Cliff Hayes of Aurora, contacted me completely out of the blue and told me he wanted to do an omnibus version (as opposed to a trolleybus version) of my two Lancashire dialect guides, I was as pleased as a dog with a tin tail. Well you know what I mean. . .

Over 14 years have passed since 'Lanky Spoken Here' was launched, and over ten years since the follow-up — 'Lanky Panky'. Both were out of print, but I still had requests from many people, from booksellers to Lanky ex-patriates for copies of the books. Sadly, I had to deny them — until now with the publication of 'Completely Lanky'.

This brings to a new generation the delights of the wonderfully rich dialect — salty as a chip butty sprinkled with the vinegar of dry wit and humour — which, I hope, will lead to a fresh appreciation of the language of our Lancashire forefathers.

It cannot be denied that the dialect is nowhere as strong as it was. Yet, with the tenacity of a terrier, it still clings on in pockets of resistance all over the county. Echoes of the Saxons and Norsemen who populated our county still ring down the ages in place names, accents and expressions.

It seems our native culture is being swamped under a tidal wave of violent American films, cheap Aussie soaps and junk food for junk minds. . . As I write, the movement grows stronger to Europeanise us all. The benefits or otherwise of that lie in the future.

But it will do no harm for all us Lancastrians to now and then look to our roots and remember where we came from, regardless of where we are going.

We might be going under. But we can go under laughing. . .

Dave Dutton
Ireby
Lancashire

DAVE DUTTON

Lancashire-born and bred (of course), Dave Dutton's Lanky credentials are impeccable...

He first saw the light of day in the former coal and cotton town of Atherton where, instead of following the family tradition of working d'eawn't pit or in't mill, he opted for the life of a reporter.

Joining the local *Leigh Reporter* (or the *Chronicle* as it then was), he achieved the dizzy heights of Chief Reporter before leaving to join the *West Lancs Evening Gazette* at Blackpool, thence to the *Manchester Evening News*.

A complete career change saw him doing scripts for Ken Dodd for seven years, after which he wrote for such varied TV shows as *The Two Ronnies*, *Dick Emery*, *Basil Brush*, *Little and Large*, and many more.

From writing for the box, he took to appearing on it. An inauspicious beginning as General Amin's legs in a comedy sketch led to bigger things. He progressed from extra work in scores of programmes to the bliss of a one-liner as a delivery man at Baldwin's factory in *Coronation Street* in which (as you will now doubt recall) he uttered the immortal line: "Mind your backs, please girls..."

The lines eventually got bigger (and better) until he was doing regular comedy character parts including the role of Oswald the Café Man (complete with filthy pinny) in the hit sit-com *Watching* and several parts in the *Street* culminating in the part of Jack Duckworth's barmy mate Bert Latham who, with Boomer the dog, led a fox hunt through the middle of Coronation Street. He has also appeared in films and commercials (mainly for beer) and has also worked on local radio.

Dave was also front man with top Lancashire comedy-folk group Inclognito for ten years. He has written 14 books and award-winning Lancashire dialect poetry and songs with a northern flavour which have been recorded by many singers.

In 1983, he started 'Now You're Talking' — an agency for after-dinner speakers — and now has over 250 top celebrities and after dinner speakers on his books.

He lives with his wife Lynn and son Gareth in what he calls 'the last hamlet in Lancashire' — Ireby, an idyllic spot on the edge of the (gasp) Yorkshire Dales but a comfortable couple of hundred yards within the Lancashire border.

He grows his own cabbages.

FOREWORD

Long Live Lanky! — From the county that brought you Blackpool Tower, Wigan Pier, L.S. Lowry, the Beatles, Gracie Fields, Eccles Cakes, Coronation Street, Crompton's Mule, Lancashire Cheese, Eric Morecambe, Beecham's Pills, Uncle Joe's Mint Balls, George Formby, Man United, the Grand National, The Co-op, Kathleen Ferrier, The Guardian, Frank Randle, Hot Pot, etc., etc., etc....

Nethen

Have you noticed how the planners are trying to make everywhere look the same; how the EEC daily threatens our way of life in the name of 'harmonisation' — providing jobs for a pestilence of bureaucrats; how the breweries have tried to standardise beer down to the lowest common denominator; and, horror of horrors, how you can now get Lancashire Cheese in tacky, sweaty little plastic packets?

In an age when the twin steamrollers of bureaucracy and big business attempt to crush humanity into a pliant, easily controlled economic units, a whiff of individuality is like a breath of fresh air in the stale sewers of conformity.

Within our nation are other little nations with their own idiosyncracies. *Dialect* is a stamp of individuality ... an aural hallmark unique to a particular area ... a language shaped on the lathe of everyday life and moulded by generations of tongues over centuries of loving use.

My dialect is the Lancashire dialect — 'Lanky' — a vibrant, vital, viable and vivid language, full of colour, expressiveness and warmth.

Pessimists have been predicting the death of the dialect 'sin Adam were a lad' — yet Lanky is still alive and kicking with both clogs. Language without dialect would be like fish and chips without the salt and vinegar.

Sadly, I have seen parts of the Lancashire I love taken away piecemeal ... sturdy, terraced homes demolished willy-nilly causing the break-up of established communities, with a resultant evaporation of neighbourliness; town centres flattened and unimaginatively homogenised; the coal and cotton industries wrung dry and thrown aside like an old dishcloth; chunks hacked off the county by overpaid bureaucrats who know little of

Lancashire and care even less; old pubs demolished or tarted up; Blackpool's Golden Mile denuded of its character; Manchester's living heart ripped out ... and I could go on. But never mind.

'We've seen Lancashire up
And seen Lancashire deawn,
Though we know that King Cotton
Has lost his gowd creawn.
Well we're nor beaten yet,
We'll beawnce back, I'll be beawnd,
'Cos we're Lancashire,
Lancashire's own!'

Dave Dutton

Dedicated to my son Gareth Dutton

CONTENTS

A Lancashire Greeting

"'Ow arta owd love?"
"Well – Ah'm noan so weel but what Ah met be better
an' Ah'm noan so bad but what Ah met bi wuss."
   Chuck thi cap in – an' cum insahd!

The Lanky Definite Article

There is *no* Lanky definite article. Merely substitute a small half-strangled explosion of air from the back of the throat. Therefore, 'down the colliery' will become **'deawn pit'.** Master this and you have mastered the first basic rule of speaking Lanky.

Basic (but not too basic) Expressions

Aye Yes	**Now** No	**Yah** and **Nay** Yes and No (when contradicting)
Sithee Behold	**Eigh Up** Hello/Well I never/Please move	**Tha wa'?** Pardon?
Dust? Do you?	**Ast?** Have you?	**Art?** Are you?
Uz'll We will	**Worrell** What will	**Them'll** They will
Owdonabit Just one moment please	**Worrizit?** Can I help you?	**Speighk proper** You are not using the correct Lancashire vernacular

2

Put-Downs

If there's one thing a Lancastrian can't abide, it's pomposity.

When in Lancashire, beware – because no matter who you are, whatever high opinion you might hold of yourself or whatever your status in life, the natives have phrases which will cut you down to size quicker than a streaker in a sawmill.

How would you like to be on the receiving end of any of the following?

Get back int' cheese – there's a maggot short!
(Be off with you, you insignificant little person!)

Who knitted *thy* face an' dropped a stitch?
(You're hardly Robert Redford, are you?)

Worrart gooin't' do fer a face when King Kong wants his arse back?
(Try going round with a bag over your head.)

Eigh up – peighs've getten their yeds above sticks ...
(These people have got ideas above their station.)

There's no show wi'out Punch.
(This person likes being the centre of attraction.)

It's a good job thi balls are in a bag.
(What a shocking memory you have, sir.)

'Er's like Blackpoo' – *everybody's* been there ...
(She is very free with her favours.)

Theaw weren't born – somebody grotched (spat) on t'waw (wall) and t' sun hatched thi eawt ...
(You weren't conceived in the normal way.)

Thi face is lahk me backside – best eawt o' seet.
(Your face is like my bottom – it should be well hidden.)

3

Oi missis – tha favvers a fairy on a muck midden!
(A cry to an overdressed woman.)

Th'art too slow ter catch a cowd. (cold).
(Do hurry up.)

Th'art nowt burra slopstone blonde.
(I perceive that your hair is bleached. A Grade A
put-down – the slopstone is an old-fashioned
Lancashire stone sink, whence the insult intimates
the colour of the insultee's hair was obtained.)

Thez a face lahk a line o' wet washin'.
(Stop sulking!)

Serves yer right fer playin' Hide-the-Sausage!
(Cry in church to an expectant bride.)

What dust think it is – charity wick? (week).
(You are presuming too much upon my good nature.)

Thaz moor chance o' gerrin' knighted, serry.
(You have little chance of achieving your objectives.)

**Anybody who sees *thee* in t' dayleet 'ull ne'er want
run away wi' thi in t' dark.**
(You're an ugly devil, aren't you?)

When Ah want monkey, Ah'll poo' t' string.
(Shut up.)

Whose turn is it ter be 'aunted toneet?
(You have a rather dishevelled appearance, madam.)

**Ah've seen moor 'air on bacon than thaz geet on thi
yed. (head).**
(You are going a bit thin on top.)

Tha'd be tall if thi feet weren't turned up so far.
(May I call you Shorty?)

Tha cawn't expect owt weer there is nowt.
(You are a brain short.)

4

Tha favvers tha's seen thi own arse.
(Do cheer up!)

Owd Mon! Th'art making a noise lahk a Co-op 'orse!
(Sir, your tendency to make loud splashing noises in
the lavatory stalls is very off-putting to the other
gentlemen using the facilities.)

**If Ah rendered thi deawn, Ah wuddn't get enought
lard fer t' oil a pair o' spectacle 'inges.**
(How painfully thin you are.)

If thi wit were shit, tha'd be constipated.
(You are not as devastatingly funny as you seem to
think you are.)

**When tha dees, con Ah 'ave bone eawt thi nose fer a
coathanger?**
(When you expire, your prominent nose bone would be
handy in my wardrobe.)

When Ah want *thy* opinion, Ah'll pull t' chain.
(Keep your nose out of my business.)

Yon mon's too numb to know he *is* numb...
(He is so unintelligent, he hasn't the intellectual
capacity to comprehend how unintelligent he really is.
A Catch 22 situation.)

If brains were a disease, tha'd be plump-i'-fettle.
(You're no mastermind, are you?)

Ah've seen better yeds on a pint of ale...
(What a dim so and so you are.)

**Th'art not fowest mon Ah've ever seen, but tha favvers
'im...**
(Granted, you are not the ugliest fellow I have
encountered, but you look like him.)

Useful Equipment to Take on Your Expedition to Deepest Lancashire

STOUT PAIR OF CLOGS – as frequently used by Lancashire philosophers for putting across the point of an argument.

SAW – for sawing knocker-upper's pole in half when you fancy a lie-in in the morning.

SHOVEL – handy for shovelling coal out of hotel bath before filling with water.

NEEDLE AND COTTON – useful for sewing your ears back on with after arguing with a Rugby League prop-forward in a pub.

SMALL TERRIER – useful for shoving down your trousers in case a ferret runs up your leg.

MACKINTOSH, WELLINGTONS, UMBRELLA, LIFE-BELT – in case the weather takes a turn for the better.

CHIP PAN – which Lancastrians use on their heads as crash-helmets.

PHOTOGRAPH OF YORKSHIREMAN – for making black puddings easier to eat: it scares them out of their skins.

ST BERNARD DOG WITH BARREL OF BEST BITTER ROUND NECK – in case you get stranded all night on a slag heap.

WHIPPET-BITE SERUM – for people who go round biting whippets.

Lanky Table Etiquette – Some Do's and Dont's

They do things differently in Lancashire. To a Lancastrian, lunchtime is *dinnertime* and dinnertime is *teatime*. Got that?

It is very important to remember that if invited to someone's home for dinner, you go at lunchtime, whereas if it's a teatime invitation, you go at dinnertime. Otherwise, if you're not careful, you could end up with no dinner at 'teatime', no lunch at 'dinnertime' – and tea with just about everything.

MANNERS

When slurping soup, do try to keep the noise down to reasonable proportions, i.e. slightly less than that of Concorde taking off.

Never drink brown sauce straight from the bottle – you never know who may have been drinking out of it before you.

Do not flick mushy peas at the waiter to attract his attention – they may stick in his ears and he won't be able to hear your order.

Do you leave a tip? Of course – no one likes eating in a tip.

It is not the done thing in Lancashire to cool one's red-hot tea by blowing on it in the cup. The correct procedure is to pour it into the saucer and fan it gently with a cloth-cap.

7

Always make sure of what you are eating – if the brown bread turns out to be hard, it could be that you've just buttered and eaten three table-mats.

When eating black puddings, always use fingers – preferably your own. Never wipe your greasy fingers on the tablecloth – stroke the dog under the table instead.

You can safely drink the water. Most Lancastrians enjoy drinking water in huge quantities – usually in conjunction with hops and malted barley.

Never use a napkin – tuck the tablecloth into your collar instead. That way, if you inadvertently drop a slippy length of tripe, it will slither its own way down back on to the plate.

EATING OUT IN LANCASHIRE
Yisluv?
I am ready to take your order, sir

Mi bally thinks me throoat's cut
I am ready to eat something

Ah cud eight a scabby pig beawt bread
Ah cud eight a flock bed
Ah cud eight a keaw (cow) **between two bread vans**
I am extremely hungry

Shape thi-sel
Harry up serree
Waiter – please act with more celerity

Ah'm o'er-faced
The abundance of food has taken away my appetite

This is gradely snap/jackbit/meight
This is good food

Yon's brunt to a frazzle
The food is burnt

Fotch three cheers
There are three of us
We require three chairs

Yon steak's as big as a fly's left nadger
They give small portions in this establishment

That's reyther moorish
I could eat more of that

Ah wur fair clemm't
I was rather peckish

Eeza proper tay-belly
My friend is very fond of tea

Stop thi' golloppin' – there's two prahzes
Take your time with the food

Stop slavverin'
Please keep your mouth from watering

Wheerst petty?
Could you direct me to the convenience?

Babbies yeds		**Blanket-lifters**
(Babies heads)		Baked Beans
Steak puddings		

| **Prayter-cakes** | **Slavvery duck** | **Feesh** |
| Potato cakes | Savoury duck | Fish |

| **Shive's o' bread** | **Dooerstep** | **Beighultam** |
| Slices of bread | Thick slice of bread | Boiled ham |

Sawt
Salt

Maggy-ann
Margarine

Barm joe
Barm cake

Crusses
Crusts

Pidjin peighs
Black peas – a
tasty Lanky dish
seen at fairs

Tommy-taters
Tomatoes

Pobs
Pieces of bread
in hot milk

Sturrer
Sterilised milk

Keaw milk
Cow milk –
pasteurised

Tin-lally butty
Sweet tinned-milk sandwich

Singing lily
Flat cake
crammed with
currants

**Corporation
pop**
Water

Gracie chips
Greasy chips

Waiter!
Bring me a glass of water – quick

This tay's like cricket pee
This tay's too wake (weak) **come eawt o't pot**
This tea is not very strong

Side table
Waiter, you may clear the table

Ah'm stawed
I am full up

Owtelse?
Do you require anything else, sir?

Yer con shuv it wheer't munkeys shuv their nuts
I disagree with your estimate of my bill, waiter

Road Signs

Motorists beware!
Here are some of the road signs peculiar to Lancashire.

You are now entering Manchester –
please open umbrella.

Southern Jessies beware – strong
Northern beer (brewer's droop zone).

Stop!

Fly over.

11

Pennine Road to Bradford – beware
sacred cows.

All Southerners must be accompanied
by their mums.

Gents, please refrain from leaving
lavvy board up.

Motorists – beware motor-cyclists on
black peas.

Beware – ferrets on heat.

Look out for pedestrians with rickets.

**DRIVE SLOWLY
– COBBLED MOTORWAY**

**WATCH OUT
– MOTHER-IN-LAW
AHEAD . . .**

**YORKSHIRE CRICKET FANS
AFTER LOSING ROSES
MATCH**

**BEWARE – RACING PIGEONS
OVERHEAD !**

**PEDESTRIAN
CLOGDANCING . . .**

**LANCASHIRE CRICKET FANS
AFTER WINNING ROSES
MATCH**

**LANCASHIRE WELCOMES
SOUTHERN DRIVERS**

ROAD SIGNS

You will encounter a number of strange road signs whilst travelling around Lancashire. Here are some to keep your eyes open for . . .

TOILETS

**YOU ARE ILLEGALLY
PARKED ON A RUGBY
LEAGUE PITCH**

**LAST BLACK PUDDING STOP
BEFORE M.1.**

13

At the Public House*

The taproom of a public house is one of the greatest repositories of Lancashire dialect. It is a place where the Lancashire man feels most at his ease and the dialect flows along with the ale. To hear Lanky **spokken proper** and see the native in his natural element, visit a taproom.

Freeman's ale's best
That beer is best which is bought for one

Ahm brastin fer a sup
I am extremely thirsty

A pahnt o' flatrib
A pint of dark mild

A jill o' bit-ther
A half-pint of bitter

Geeuza pahnt o' girder
I would like a pint of Guinness, landlord.
(This drink is reputed to have tumescent properties)

Bones
Dominoes

Arrers
Darts

Bowels
Crown green bowls
(also known as **woods**)

This ale's aw reet fur purrin' on chips
Landlord, your beer tastes like vinegar

14

Don't sup that, it'll blow thi bally-button off
Put that keg beer down

A breawn split
Brown ale mixed with bitter or mild

This ale tastes lahk maiden's-waiter
It is extremely weak

It's lahk gnat-pee
Like I said – it's extremely weak

Wiv stopped some ale fra gooin' seawr
Wiv ginnit some stick
We have consumed a goodly quantity of beer

'Ee's takkin a sweetener wom
He is taking home a bottle of beer in order to
ingratiate himself with his wife, because he has been
out too long

Ee's a reet ale-can
He is a potential alcoholic

Brewer's goitre
Pot-belly

Backer
Tobacco

Smooks
Cigarettes

Ee smooks lahk a fackthry chimbley
He smokes like a factory chimney

They'n signed him 'igh
He's been banned *sine die* from a club

Ee's playin' him
He has absconded from work

Ah'm short o' dosh
I have no money

Ah've ad a boatload
I'm full of beer

This is fer 'oo kissis Betty
This is to decide who is the overall winner (at darts, dominoes, etc)

Ahm on a promise
My wife has promised me her sexual favours

It's lahk payin' to a chance-child
The price of this beer is extortionate

'Is tap's stopped
The landlord is refusing to serve him
His wife is denying him his conjugal rights

Ee's no clack in 'im
His legs is 'oller
He is a prodigious drinker

It's a smookjack/smooker
That was marvellous
(of a good dart/goal/bowl, etc)

Yer con bet Connie's odds
Nothing is more certain

Ah'll gam on it
I will bet money on it

Gerreminagen!
Landlord, please replenish our glasses!

Eez spewed iz ring up
He has been sick all over the carpet
(otherwise known as 'shouting for Hughie' after the
'EEOOIE!' sound it makes)

Speak up Brown – you're through!
Said after someone has 'broken wind,' 'dropped
one,' 'cut their finger,' 'let Polly out of prison',
'trumped,' etc.

**She'll do it fer peanuts then come back fer't
shells**
A reference to a woman of loose morals

It came away like a flock o' sparrows
A reference to loose bowels

17

Ee's peed aw 'is munny agenst waw
He has spent all his money on beer

Sod this fer a game o'sowjers
I don't intend carrying on along these lines

Chukkin eawt tahm
Closing time

Avyernowomsgutto?!
Time gentlemen, please!

Ah'll see thi't morn morn
I'll see you tomorrow morning

Ah've bin ta'n short
I will have to go to the toilet

That's peed on't chips
That's very unfortunate

Strap it
I will pay for it at a later date

Ah must empty mi' clog
Ah'm gooin fert shake honds wi't best mon at mi weddin'
Ah'm gooin't shake dew off me lily
Ah'm brastin fer a slash
I simply must visit the gents

Pie-eyed . . . Slat at . . . Kalied . . . Piddelt . . . Slewed ter't gills . . . Tanked up . . . Sozzlt . . . Skennin moppin' drunk
Drunk!

Ee's drunk uz a fiddler's foo
Ee's drunk as a mop
Ee's drunk as a monkey
Ee's getten a sweigh on
He is extremely drunk

Insults

Tha'rt as thick as a Wiggin butty
Tha'rt as dim as a TocH lamp
Tha'rt thick as pigmuck
Tha'rt numm as a pit-prop
You seem to have a very low I.Q.

Th'art nowt an' nowt'll become o' thi an' aw thi
'air'll drop eawt
You are very wicked and you will come to nothing
and all your hair will drop out
(a frightening warning of a semi-prophetic nature
to a bad person)

Thezza mahnd like a muck-midden
You are of a coarse nature

Thezza yedfull o' jolly robins
You are nothing but a daydreamer

Yurra big tatah
You are somewhat effeminate

Ah'm tawkin tert th'organ-grahnder – norriz
munkey
Ah'm tawkin tert th'enjin-drahver – norriz
rubbin-rag
You are of no consequence – I am speaking to
people who know more about these things than
you do

He con get wheer weyter cawnt
He can get where water can't
(i.e. everywhere; a half-grudging, half-jealous remark of a person who does well through his efforts
at dealing with people)

21

Thurr nowt burra load o' rang-tang
They are a rubbishy bunch of fellows

Art tryin't pee up mi back?
Are you trying to arouse my temper?

When theaw wur born, thi shudda kept th'after-birth an thrown't babby away
The midwife who brought you into the world did it a disservice

Thaz too much o' that what cat licks its bottom wi'
You talk too much

Ee'd skin a flea for awpni.
Ee wuddn't gi thi't steam offizpee
If eeda gobful o' gumbeighls, e wuddn't part wi' one
That man is mean

Ee wouldn't pee on you if you wur burnin'
He is not a very helpful fellow

Pig off, yer greyt eggwap
You are a fool – please go away

Stop thi' tollerin
Desist from showing off

Huh – theer guz Little Miss Keck
That girl is very forward

Ah bet thy teeth're glad when tha'rt asleep
You don't half talk a great deal

Who's getten thee ready?
Insulting remark to a well-dressed person

Ee thinks its fer sturrin' iz tay with
He thinks it's for stirring his tea with.
(a slighting reference to a sexually inexperienced male)

Ee's proper monkified
He is very mischievous

'Ee's as useless as a one-legged mon at an arse-kickin' contest
He is *very* useless

Tell't trooth an shoam't divil
Tell the truth and shame the devil
You tell lies

Tha'rt proper mard thy art
You are spoiled and childish

Gutter hell an' pump at thunder
Shove off

Bumpin' weight
A curious adjectival term usually tagged on to an obscene noun

Tha'rt an idle scrawp
You are a lazy so-and-so

The following names all mean roughly the same thing, i.e. a fool, and should only be used when speaking to a person of a much smaller stature (preferably a one-legged midget), or when the person delivering the insult can boast some degree of efficiency in the martial arts:

Tha'rt nowt burra . . .
You are nothing but a . . .

Slavverin' foo	**Snowbaw**	**Snorin' crow**
Crate-egg	**Warpyed**	**Rubbin rag**
Noan reet bugga	**Bladder-yed**	**Bun-yed**
Stonejug	**Eighl-can**	**Gobshite**

There, you've said it – now run like blazes!

Alphabetical Disorder

Forget all they ever taught you at primary school...it's time to re-learn the alphabet - Lanky style.

When it comes to pronunciation, letters of the Lanky alphabet do not abide by the usual accepted rules of Standard English. They change peculiarly when translated into Lanky. For instance:

A can = **E** - as in seck (sack) or mek (make) or tek (take). (Art tekkin' it in?)

But, A can also = **O** - as in 'ond (hand) or sond (sand) or mon (man). Cont understond it?

Ah, but O can also = **U** - in certain words; eg. a dog is a dug, a man called Tom is Tum and clogs are clugs. (Don't get it wrung).

And what is more, I can end up as E as when string becomes sthreng, light becomes leet and night becomes neet. (Aw reet?)

To confuse the matter further, when it comes to the letter H the Lancastrian **doesn't** use it when he **should,** and **does** use it when he **shouldn't** - as in "Ah wur as 'ungry as an 'orse but Ah've only heaten a hegg with a horange fer hafters". (Hokay so far?)

What is even stranger, the letters D and T acquire H's from nowhere which is enoof ter mek sthrung lurry dhreivurs weep. (Is it dhreivin' yer daft?)

And while we're at it, the Lanky letter R sometimes jumps one place to the left of its own accord as in brast for burst and brunt for burnt. (Is that clear, owd brid?)

And finally, but most importantly, whether it's Christmas or not, the Lanky Alphabet sometimes has "No L" "No L" - as in words like call, fall, wall and ball used as "When Ah heard mi mam caw, Ah fawed off t' waw an' dropped mi baw..."
AN' THAT'S AW!

Useful Abuseful Phrases

It's as well to know when you are being insulted in Lancashire. Though usually extremely hospitable, the native Lancastrian can become aggressive when he considers you have offended his honour – such as by knocking over his pint pot or driving over his favourite pet whippet.

Here are some of the things he may say to you.

(*NB*. Using any of the following to a fair-sized Lancastrian is a quick way of finding out at first-hand the quality of hospital food in the county.)

Dust want a leather 'n' timber kiss?
(How do you fancy a kick from my clog?)

Ah'll tek a bit o' thi wom (home) in me pocket.
(There'll be bits of you missing when I've finished!)

Thaz a face lahk a constipated bloodhound!
(Smile, please.)

If tha'd hafe a brain, tha'd be an ape.
(You are somewhat deficient in grey matter.)

Th'art purrin' (putting) thi yed in a dog kennel!
(Don't mess about with me or you'll get in trouble.)

Tha favvers tha's bin punched gether.
(You look slightly deformed.)

Tha skens (squints) enoof ter crack a lookin'-glass.
Tha skens enoof ter upset an 'orse an' cart.
Tha skens lahk a basket o' whelks.
(Remarks to one with cross-eyes.)

Ah'll gi thi some clog toe pie.
(Not an invitation to dinner – this is an offer to give you a good kicking.)

Thaz a nose lahk a blind cobbler's thumb!
(Your nose is a funny shape!)

Th'art nor 'avvin' *me* **on a butty.**
(Don't try it on with me.)

Ah'll snatch thi breath!
(I'll kill you!)

Ah'll tek it eawt thi ribs!
(Pay what you owe me or I'll have the satisfaction of giving you a good hiding!)

Art tawkin' ter me or chewin' a brick?
(You are conversing rather indistinctly.)

Ast getten a feather up thi arse?
(Remark to one laughing over-excessively.)

Dust wanna faceful o' dandruff?
(This refers to a butt in the face. In Lanky, a butt is also known as a tup - also the name colloquially given to a ram because of its habit of butting. Thus, the town of *Ramsbottom* is known as Tup's Arse.

Ah'll lamp thi yerrole!
(I will hit you in the ear!)

Th'art too fow t' make arse'oles on - warty uns.
(You are too ugly to make anuses out of - not even work-day ones. "Warty" has nothing to do with warts - it means workday: as in "warty clothes" (workday clothes) as opposed to Sunday best. Thus the insult infers that the person referred to is not even fit material for fashioning the most inferior kind of anus - a double insult!)

Tha makes me bum wink.
(I am fed up with you.)

I hope thi balls turn square an' fester at corners.
(A fate too terrible to dwell upon.)

If thi brains were made o' gunpowder, there wouldn't be enough ter part thi' 'air.
(You're obviously an idiot.)

Who rattled t'side o' *thy* hutch?
(When I want your advice, I'll ask for it...)

Ah wouldn't wash *thy* underpants fer £1 a rub.
(You are breaking wind somewhat excessively.)

'E's so mean that when he gets up of a mornin', 'e looks under t' bed fer t' see if 'e's lost any sleep.
(He's an old Scrooge.)

Fighting Talk*

*FEIGHTIN'TAWK

On yer bike!
Despatch yourself hence!

Tha'll cop it neaw
You are for it my friend

Th'art nowt a peawnd
You are nothing-a-pound
I am not afraid of you

Ah'll spit in thi eye an' bugblind thi
I am about to become aggressive

There's moor bant in a wet lettuce
You are a weakling, sir

Ah'll banjo thee
You have no chance against my superior fighting
powers

Dust want a knuckle butty?
Would you like to taste my fist?

Tha's a face lahk a joss–arsed baboon
You are no oil-painting, sir

Ah'll cleawt thi' lug'ole
I am aiming for your ear

Ah'll mollycrush thee
I will totally annihilate you

Ah'll parr thi' yed in
I intend to cave your cranium in

Ah'll paste thi ear'ole
I'll flatten your ear for you

Th'art as fow as a gasmon's mac
You are as ugly as a gas meter reader's attire

**If 'ee 'ad any moor meawth, 'eed 'ave no face
left ter wesh**
If his mouth was any bigger, he would have no face
left to wash

Eez lahk a dog wi' a tin dick
Eez lahk a dog wi' two dicks
He is extremely pleased

Gerrim gelded!
Drastic measures are needed to curb him

**If tha doesn't gerrup quick, I'll cum'n pee in thi
earhole!**
Shouted upstairs as an encouragement for someone
to get out of bed

Ahlommerthi
I will hammer you

Ah'll beeyit thi
I will beat you

Ah'll skutch thi legs
I will scrape your legs

Tha cuddn't lick a toffee apple
You've no chance

Choose thi winder
I am giving you the
opportunity of picking
the window you wish me
to throw you through

Dust wanna Wigan Kiss?
Would you like me to butt you in the face?

Ah'll punch thi supper up
This next blow is aimed at your abdomen

Dustgeeup?
Have you had enough?

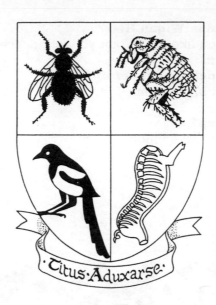

·Titus·Aduxarse·

The Yorkshire Coat of Arms

As most people know, Yorkshire is a little place just
outside Lancashire. A Yorkshireman is merely a failed
Lancastrian and his emblem is a red rose suffering
from anaemia.

At Rugby League matches, the Yorkshire contingent
yell at the Lancashire crowd: "Lancashire Hot Pots!"
To which the Lancashire spectators respond with
"Yorkshire *Puddings*!" They never learn.

Here is the official Yorkshire coat of arms, as found
on the walls of Payfersod Hall, just outside
Heckmondwike...

As you can see, this contains a fly, a flea, a magpie
and a side of bacon...

Reasons for this are obvious. A fly will sup with
anybody – and so will a Yorkshireman. A flea will
bite anybody – and so will a Yorkshireman. A magpie
will chatter with anybody – and so will a
Yorkshireman. And a side of bacon is never any good
until it's been hanged...

31

Alltergetheragen!

Lancashire words are like fish and chips – they go together. Sometimes, a whole sentence can be telescoped to form one word bearing no resemblance to spoken English.

Try getting your teeth round these....

Sawreetferthee.
(It is all right for you.)

Erzfawnwityedintpo.
(She has tripped and landed with her head in the chamber-pot.)

Eezertizont.
(He has injured his hand.)

Yonzeez.
(That belongs to him.)

Erzurzawlowerer.
(She is in dire need of a depilatory cream.)

Geeuzakisswilta?
(Would you give me a kiss?)

Astbrowtitwithi?
(Have you brought it with you?)

Izziterzerizziteez?
(Does it belong to her or does it belong to him?)

Eeeyafflaff.
(You have to laugh, don't you?)

Azzertannerpuss? **Fotchiteerserry.**
(Has she taken her purse?) (Please bring it here, sir)

Izyedzawshapes.
(He has a lumpy cranium.)

Avaddabuttifermitay.
(I have had a sandwich for tea.)

Astastaskastaskter?
(I shall have to ask – have you asked her?)

Interfow?
(Isn't she ugly?)

Ahlsithitmornmornermornneet.
(I will either see you tomorrow morning or tomorrow night.)

Corpcartkektoeranthorstukboggarts!
(The cart belonging to the Co-operative Society fell over and the horse ran off in fright!)

The (Secret) Shibboleths

No matter how good a foreigner (ie. a Southern jessie) becomes at aping the Lanky lingo, there are certain words which will always catch him out and brand him an outsider. These are the secret shibboleths – "shibboleth" being the word that the Ephraimites could not say correctly when challenged to do so by their enemies the Gileadites.

If you wish to perfect your pronunciation of Lanky sufficiently to mingle unnoticed among Lancastrians, take special note of the following:-

A garage is not a gar-ahj – it is a *garridge.*
Mauve is never mohve but *mawve.*
A bus is not a bass but a *buzz.*
A piece of nougat is not a piece of noo-gar but a piece of *nuggit.*
Envelopes are not onvelopes but *e*nvelopes.
A room is not a rum.
Awmonds are olmonds.
A scone is not a sco*h*ne – it's a sconn.
A tortoise is definitely not a tortus – it is a *toytoyse.*
So be warned.

Ignore these pronunciations at your peril. And if you don't know what happened to the Ephraimites...see JUDGES XII.

Look Out – It's the L.C.P!

Question: What is a Lancashire lad?

Answer: "The genuine Lancashire lad is a being
worthy of study. His deep sense of humour; his
patient endurance of adversity; his lifelong struggle
with want; his indomitable perserverance; his love of
home – all point him out as one of a remarkable race.
And despite his sometimes rough exterior and uncouth
language, your real Lancashire lad is one of nature's
gentlemen at heart." So wrote William E. A. Axon in
his book *Folk Song and Folk Speech of Lancashire*
many years ago.

What he *definitely* wasn't talking about was that
heartstopping horror the Lanky Chauvinist Pig.

Here is some help in identifying him...though if
you ever meet an LCP, you won't need any clues –
you'll *know*...

The Lanky Chauvinist Pig has an IQ of 27 with his
flat cap on – and 12½ with it off. The LCP is one of
the species that Darwin missed. He is a quaint
anachronism, a throwback to the Dark Ages, a slight
hiccup in Mother Nature's grand scheme of things. In
other words, he's a right pillock.

He is a man of few needs. Observe, the Lancashire
Handkerchief – or the Lanky Hanky...

Which he uses, thus –

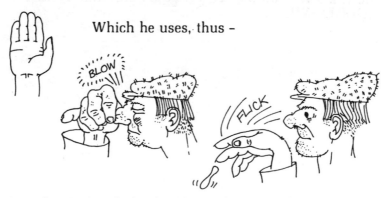

Moral: *Never* shake hands with a Lanky Chauvinist
Pig...

To preserve his manhood in the eyes of other LCPs, he would never be seen dead carrying any of the following in his hand:
(a) A bunch of flowers; (b) a gill (half-pint) glass of ale; (c) an umbrella; (d) a poetry book; (e) his wife's coat. To be seen by cronies carrying any of these would qualify him instantly for Gay Lib.

LCP wives never nag their husbands in bed. If they are tempted to do so, retribution is swift as the LCP practises his own method of administering an anaesthetic by forcing his wife's head under the sheets and breaking wind. Thus ensuring a good night's sleep

(for him if not his wife).

The LCP has a unique and infallible way of slimming. When he staggers home from the pub, he picks up his dinner and throws it at the wall – thus at one stroke cutting down his calories and saving on washing-up liquid. (Some LCP wives inured to this dinner-slinging have become adept at eating the meal with a knife and fork as it's sliding down the wallpaper).

The LCP firmly believes in a working-man's right to strike – his mother-in-law, in the teeth.

The LCP always has a warm welcome for Yorkshire folk – he sets fire to their trouser-legs.

He has scrupulous standards of hygiene – he always insists on spraying his whippets with DDT before allowing them in bed with him and the wife.

The LCP is very possessive. To ensure nobody touches his beer when he goes to the pub lavatory, he places his false teeth in his pint. (This is also a standard gambit for acquiring the ale of unsuspecting southern jessies.)

When walking through the park or grassland, the LCP always allows his wife to precede him by three paces. This ensures that whatever's lurking his wife stands in it first – whereupon he executes a sidestep.

The LCP thinks that a rank outsider is a southern jessie with BO. But he'll always oblige him with an exhibition of clogdancing – usually on top of his head.

How to Recognise a Lanky Chauvinist Pig (L.C.P.)

He always carries two short planks under his arm to illustrate what he thinks a Yorkshireman is as thick as.

Though Lancastrians are by nature warm and friendly – unlike the climate – as in any society, you may meet the occasional bigot who is ill-disposed to outsiders – usually Southern '*jessies*' and Yorkshire '*puddings*.' I have christened such a being the Lanky Chauvinist Pig. This is how to recognise him:

He uses toilet-paper with pictures of Eddie Waring, Michael Parkinson and Geoff Boycott on.

He never asks your opinion about Lancashire – he *tells* you.

His wife always walks three paces behind him – with a big whip in her hand.

He has a soft spot for Southerners – the quicksands at Morecambe Bay.

He breaks wind loudly, then blames it on the dog.

He thinks the ideal method of birth control is keeping a ferret in bed.

He reckons the chip-pan is the greatest invention since the wheel.

That's him drinking *your* ale. . . .

"Philosophy"

Lancashire folk have a great deal of commonsense –
the fact that they live in Lancashire proves that. Thus,
the visitor will often encounter some homespun
philosophy proffered by some Wigan Socrates or
Ramsbottom's answer to Plato.

If you do not understand the deep fundamental
truths the philosopher is trying to convey, don't
worry. The chances are that neither does he...

Ponder the following:-

A meawse what's nobbut one 'ole's soon takken.
(A mouse with only one hole to run to is soon caught.
One should always have more than one avenue of
escape in any situation.)

The minutes tha plays thi, tha'll ne'er 'aft work.
(The moments of time you have had off work have
gone and you will never have to work them.)

**'Ard work never killed anybody. It's made 'em some
bloody funny shapes.**
(The second sentence indicates some reluctance to
believe in the truth of the first.)

Them az az _will_ 'ave.
(Fortune usually smiles on those who don't need it.)

A creakin' door'll 'ang a good while on its 'inges.
(Invalids usually have long lives.)

All is not gold that glitters – an' all is not shit that smells.
(Don't be fooled by appearances – of _any_ shape.)

Tha doesn't look at mantelpiece when th'art pokin' t' fire.
(You don't have to look at an ugly girl's face when
you're enjoying yourself with her.)

A bee in a cow-turd thinks himsel a King.
(An upstart-deflater.)

Ah con do owt except wheel misel in a barrow.
(There are limits to one's capabilities.)

One tale's good till another's towd. (told).
(A one-sided story always sounds plausible – until
you hear the other side. Witness party political
broadcasts.)

**A fool con ask moor questions in five minutes than a wise
mon con answer in a month.**

Them as beighs (buy) beef beighs bones,
Them as beighs land beighs stones,
Them as beighs eggs beighs shells,
But them as beighs good ale beighs nowt else!
(Perhaps that's why we like our ale so much in
Lancashire.)

The Wick, The Dead – and The Poorly Sick Wi' A Shawl on...

In a Lancashire household, whenever the local newspaper plops on the mat, the first page that is generally turned to is the one containing the obituary column.

The latest gossip about "whooz deed?" and "whooz on 'iz road eawt?" provides great fuel for discussion among the local community.

Here then are some "dead good" phrases to make you fain t' bi wick (glad to be alive)...

Tha favvers thaz bin dug up.
(You have the pallor of a corpse.)

Ah'm only walkin' abeawt fer t' save buryin'-brass 'cos Ah cawn't afford dee.
(The only reason I'm alive is that I am so poor I can't afford the money to be interred.)

Ah'm proper poorly sick wi' a shawl on.
(I'm really ill.)

'Eez dropped off perch.
'Eez popped 'is clogs.
'Eez cocked 'is toes.
Gone dee-erd.
(He is now the deceased.)

If 'eez tan (taken) aw 'is brass wi' 'im, it'll aw bi melted bi neaw.
(You can bet *he* hasn't gone to heaven.)

'E never 'ad a doctor – 'e deed 'uv 'imself.
(He died naturally – he didn't need a doctor's help to do so.)

Wudta be as sharp in mi grave?
(A sarcastic remark to someone who takes over someone's place on a seat very quickly.)

Cheer up – there's awlus lodge.
(A cheerful encouragement to commit suicide – a lodge is a stretch of water beside a factory.)

Th'art too awkert dee.
(You are too obstinate to expire.)

Simithry.
(Cemetery.)

T' Divil's 'ad porridge and t' Lord's nobbut getten pon fer t' scrape.
(Said of a deathbed repentance when someone has led a sinful existence...ie The Devil's had all the porridge and God's only got the pan to scrape.)

Tha looks pot.
(You look out of sorts.)

'Eez getten a wooden top-cooert. (top-coat).
(He is in a coffin.)

Tha'll never live ter scratch a grey yed!
(You won't live long enough to collect your pension!)

Th'art awluvva wacker.
Th'art wackerin' lahk a tripe doll.
(You are trembling a great deal.)

Never – till Ah'm lyin' on mi back between two pieces o' wood wi' mi gob full o' sond (sand)!
(A Lanky version of "Over my dead body!")

'Ee'd bi wuss (worse) if owt ailed 'im.
(There isn't a thing wrong with him.)

'Ast played a wrong domino?
(Said to someone with a broken leg, this alludes to the proliferation of cheats at dominoes. When a "bad" domino is played by their partners, they give them a hefty kick under the table to draw attention to their mistake.)

43

And some Lanky remedies...

To rid yourself of earwarch (earache): spit in your ear.
To rid yourself of a pimple: rub saliva on it.
To banish a wart: tie a horse's hair round it or sell it
for sixpence.
To cure yedwarch (headache): dip a rag in vinegar and
water and wrap round head.
To ward off rheumatism: keep a nutmeg in your pocket.
To alleviate swollen glands: boil a potato in its skin,
place it in a sock and wrap the sock round your neck.
A facetious "cure" for constipation: shove an umbrella
up and bring it down open!

Visiting the Doctor

Are theaw't quack?
Excuse me, are you the doctor?

Ah feel wake
I feel weak

Ah keep gooin' mazey
I am continually having dizzy spells

Ah'm aw cowd crills
I am shivering

Ah varnear collopst
I have nearly collapsed

Ah'm reet jiggered
I am tired out through effort

Ah'm eawt o' flunther
I feel out of condition
(this word is also used to denote some piece of
apparatus is not functioning)

Ah'm cowfin lahk a good-un
I can't seem to stop coughing

Ah'm powfagged
I'm weary/browbeaten

Ah'm up stick
I think I am pregnant

Ah'm too double wi't bellywarch
I'm doubled up with stomach pains

Ah've getten yedwarch
My head aches

Ah'm bun up
I am constipated
(egg-bun is the state of being constipated through
eating too many eggs)

Ah cud do wi summat purra road through me
Please prescribe me a laxative
(also known as **oppenin'-medicine**)

Ah'm stuffed-up to buggery wi' a cowd
I'm full of a cold

Mi guts're off   **It's chickinpots**
I have tummy trouble   Chickenpox

Cough it up – it met be a pianner
Get it off your chest (phlegm)

It's summat an' nowt
You'll survive

Ah'm swettin' lahk a pig
I have a perspiration problem

Purruz on't club wilta?
I wish to receive National Health benefits

Ah'm ruff as a badgers arse
Ah'm a bit offside
I feel off-colour

Ees ta'n bad roads   **Ah'm still a bit tickle**
The patient is getting worse   I am still not quite right

Ah've a spile in mi ont
I have a splinter in my hand

Ah've summat in mi een
I have something in my eye

Ah feel lahk am on feigher
I am running a temperature

Mi gob tastes lahk th'inside uv a Turkish wrestler's jockstrap
I have halitosis

Ah think ahm mendin'
I am getting much better

Some Affectionate Terms

Owd Beigh . . . Owd Beighzer . . . Buggerlugs . . . Brid . . . Cocker . . . Fettler . . . Owd Lad . . . Owd Luv . . . Owd Jockey . . . Skimbo . . . Sticker . . . Owd Stockin' . . . Owd Stockin Top . . . Owd Sparrer . . . Owd Shugger Butty . . Owd Scholar . . . Owd Prater . . . Owd Prater Pie

To be used only when you have gained the utmost respect, familiarity and affection of a Lancastrian, such as when you've bought him a pint in a pub:

The word **'thee'** can be used as a term to express real affection in such phrases as **'Ee ah luv thee,'** or **'Ah've tekken ter thee.'**

But it can also be most insulting when used offensively, as when speaking to someone older than you are, or in aggressive circumstances, such as **'Oi thee – ah'll punch thi nose tert back o' thi face.'**

When used in unfortunate circumstances and the recipient feels offended, he will usually respond with **'Don't thee thee me thee'.**

A Lanky Anatomy Lesson

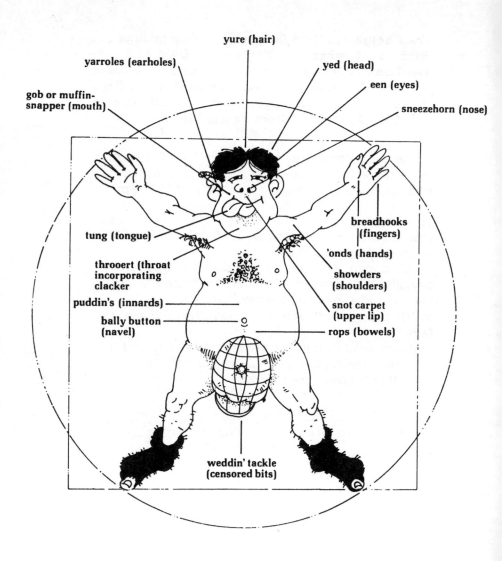

yure (hair)

yarroles (earholes)

yed (head)

een (eyes)

gob or muffin-snapper (mouth)

sneezehorn (nose)

tung (tongue)

breadhooks (fingers)

'onds (hands)

throoert (throat incorporating clacker

showders (shoulders)

puddin's (innards)

snot carpet (upper lip)

bally button (navel)

rops (bowels)

weddin' tackle (censored bits)

49

Occupations

Owd septic knuckles
The rent man

Skoomesther
Schoolmaster

Sowjer
Soldier

Wakesmon
Fairground worker

Torchy
Cinema usher

Lekkymon
Electricity meter reader

Buzz dreighvur
Bus driver

Chukker-eawter
Bouncer

Parkie
Park keeper

Clubmon
Insurance collector

Lurry dreighvur
Lorry driver

Binmon
Refuse collector

Rozzer
Policeman

Papperlad
Newsboy

Descriptions

Lanky has some biting phrases to describe people's attributes and characteristics. I sincerely hope you don't find yourself on the sharp end of any of these...

'Er could talk under-watter.
'Er could meither a nest o' rats.
'Er could talk fer Lankysher.
'Er's getten a tongue lahk a length o' tripe.
(She's a typical woman.)

'E's plaitin' 'is legs.
(He is somewhat drunk.)

'Is heels 'ave getten master uv 'is yed.
(Yes, he is definitely drunk.)

'Is nose cost as much brass fer t' paint as a row o' good-size heawses...
(He suffers from a boozer's cherry nose.)

'E wouldn't gi' a frog a jump.
'E wouldn't gi' a lavvy door a bang.
'E were born wi' cramp in 'is fist.
'E wouldn't part wi' t' smook off 'is porridge.
(He is an extremely mean man.)

'E's bowlegged wi' brass.
(He is rather well-to-do.)

'E's norra full shillin'...
'E's no oil in 'is lamp...
'E's not geet aw 'is cheers awom. (his chairs at home).
(He wouldn't make a good Prime Minister.)

'E's aw theer wi' 'is mint drops.
(He knows what's what.)

'Er's moor edge abeawt 'er than a butcher's saw.
(She's nothing but a show-off.)

She'd bend deawn to a bulldog...
(She is a little oversexed.)

**'E'd pee through somebody's letterbox, then knock on t'
door to ask heaw far it went.**
(He is a cheeky man.)

'E lahks smell of 'is own trumps.
(What a vain man he is!)

'E's etten moor than 'e gradely should.
(He hasn't left any food for anyone else.)

'E's getten no 'inge in 'is back.
(He is not a creep.)

'E's a face lahk a ruptured custard.
(He is not a pretty sight.)

'Er's poxed up ter t' eyebrows.
(She is suffering from a social disease.)

'E favvers a Red Indian.
(He looks hot and bothered.)

Ah've a bum like a cherry/lahk a blood orange.
(I was on the curry last night.)

They'n moor twists than a game o' pontoon.
(They are a very devious lot.)

He's got ten bob on 'imself...
(He holds himself in inordinately high regard.)

Th'art as much use as a balloon bowt skin.
(You are totally ineffectual.)

'Er's a face lahk a well-slapped arse.
(She has a somewhat ruddy complexion.)

'Er's getten footbaw eyes – one at 'ome and one away.
(She suffers from a pronounced squint.)

'E's a gob lahk a parish oven.
(He is very fond of the sound of his own voice.)

Tha favvers tha's fawed off a flittin'. (flitting = a house removal).
(You are an unsightly mess.)

'E wur three feet between 'is eyes!
(He was a rather large individual.)

There's moor (more) work in a glass of Andrews...
(He's one of those social security scroungers.)

Look out – there's a shirtlifter behind thee.
(A man with gay tendencies is standing to your rear.)

Thi willy must be full o' spud-wayter. (potato water).
(I fear you could be infertile.)

'Er has a face lahk a bulldog lickin' piss off a thistle...
(She has a somewhat dour countenance.)

If Ah'd a face like thine, Ah'd teach mi arse ter speak.
(God, but you're ugly!)

Features

'Ee's as thin as a Nooner wi' one meetin' in it
He's very thin
(refers to midday edition of racing-paper with only
one race meeting and therefore only a couple of
pages)

'Er's a face lahk a busted clog/a melted welly
She isn't very pretty

'Eee's as fow as a summons
He is ugly and unwanted
(**fow** can mean ugly – of a person or place – and also
lucky . . . as in **'yer fow divil,'** meaning 'you lucky
devil')

It favvers a sod reawnd a rat-hole
**Why cultivate on thi' face what grows wild
reawnd thi' arse?**
Pejorative term relating to a person's moustache

'Eigh Fatrops!
An attempt to attract a portly gentleman's attention

**'Er looks lahk a bag o' muck teed in't middle wi
a piece o' string**
Said of an unshapely woman in a dress

Snot carpet
The distance between one's nostrils and one's top
lip

Eez up and down lahk a prostitute's pants
Eez up and down lahk a fartinabottle
He is very restless

Eez lahk a fart in a cullinder
He doesn't know which way to turn

54

Eez geet eyes lahk rissoles in the snow
A euphemism for someone whose eyes have taken
on a sunken appearance

Ast getten sum muck on thi' top lip?
Asked of person with look of distate on face

Tha'art a reet toe-rag
You are a most unworthy person

Yon mon con whisper o'er three fields
That fellow has an exceptionally loud voice

'Ee walks lahk a ruptured duck
He does not walk normally

Oi Rag-eye!
I say, you with the eye defect!

'Ee's a face uz'd stond cloggin'
He is most hard-faced

He cud walk under th'essole wi a top hat on
He is very small

Tha favvers ready fer killin'
'Aven't ah seen thi' in Yates and
Greers' winder wi' an apple in
thi gob?
Insults to fat people, relating to a pig being ready
for slaughter and a pig's head in a butcher's window

Ah cud eight them beawt bread
That young lady has a buxom appearance

'Ee favvers a strake o' pee on a whiteweshed
waw
Isn't he thin?

'Er's getten sparrerlegs
She has extremely thin legs

'Eigh, thee wi't pastie-feet!
Excuse me, the gentleman with the large feet!

It's surprisin' what yer see when yer eawt beawt gun
That's a very unusual-looking person

Art breighkin' um in fer an 'orse?
Reference to large teeth

Ten ter two feet
Feet splayed out in V-shape

'Ee cudn't stop a pig in a ginnel
He is bowlegged

Shut thi gob an' gi' thi' arse a chance
I fear you are monopolising the conversation

'Ee cud carry fahve peawnd o' King Edwards iniz cap
He has an unusually large head

'Ees as randy as a booardin'-eawse tomcat
He is of an amorous nature

Az sumbdi cut thi' 'air wi a knahf un fork?
Your barber's tonsorial capabilities leave much to be desired.

'Ee int hawf ballyin' eawt
His abdomen is getting bigger

'Er's as fawce as a ferret
She is cunning

Tha'rt as black as up chimney
Why don't you have a wash?

'Ere's mi yed, mi arse is cummin
Applied to a person who walks in a bustling manner
with head to the fore

Things we say...

– Being glittering jewels of folk-wisdom that have been passed down along the ages, like mumps, scarlet fever and athlete's foot...

A shut meawth (mouth) keeps flies eawt.
(If you keep your mouth closed, you won't get in bother; so keep quiet and don't repeat others' gossip.)

Second 'un sits on t' best knee.
(The second wife of a marriage frequently gets treated better than the first one.)

'Im in t' neet wi' t' rag arm.
(Him in the night with the amputated arm – a nonsense retort for parrying inquisitive people who want to know who you are talking about.)

Muck midden pride – a carriage weddin' an' a wheelbarrow flittin'.
(The price you pay for being "showy".)

Beauty's only skin deep – but it's a bugger when tha 'ast use a *pick* ter ger at it...
(There's ugliness – and then there's *ugliness*.)

Tha met bi born but th'art not dee-erd yet.
(You might be born but you're not dead yet, ie. you might be congratulating yourself that you are doing very nicely – but a lot of nasty things could happen to you before you die, so don't be too sure of yourself.)

Better to give a shillin' than lend hawf a creawn (half-a-crown).
(If you give somebody a shilling, that's all you've lost; but if you lend somebody half-a-crown and they don't give it back, you've lost 2½ times as much.)

Th'arl come to thi cake an' milk.
(You'll get what's coming to you.)

Stopped fer bobbins.
(Out of work – or a temporary hiatus.)

Smile and t'world smiles wi' thi – cry an' tha'll pee less.
(Lancastrian philosophy.)

Tha con caw mi what tha wants, but don't caw mi late fer mi dinner.
(Insults are one thing, a proper sense of priorities another.)

Ah've no moor use fer it as a duck 'as fer an umbrella.
(I haven't any use for it whatsoever.)

It's a poor arse that can't rejoice...
Better eawt than in...
There's mony a one in t' simithry (cemetery) us'd be fain t' do that...
(Responses to comments of disapproval after someone has "broken wind".)

Tha wants aw thi own road an' a bag purrit in.
(You are spoiled.)

'Arken' t' kettle cawin' t' pon brunt arse.
(Listen to the kettle calling the pan black.)

Tha wants know tale and t' tale's master.
(You want to know the lot.)

Ah bet there's moor snotty noses than standin' pricks *this* **weather...**
(The cold snap shows no sign of abating.)

Ah've got booath feet in one clog.
(I just can't seem to get started today.)

Sayings

The traveller will frequently be bemused by various 'sayings' which the native Lancastrian is fond of trotting out, and which usually encapsulate some grain of truth.

In the event of being unable to understand the speaker, the traveller is advised to nod knowingly and sympathetically and act as though he has been the recipient of some great truth.

**Tha con treighed on't cat till it
turns on thi**
You can tread on a cat until it turns on you
You can only push a person so far

Wheer thurs least room, thurs mooerst thrutchin'
People who criticise other people should have
regard to their own faults first

A big knocker sets a dooer off
A big nose gives a face character
(usually said by people with big noses)

It's gone wheer its ned
Said grudgingly of someone who has a windfall

God's good ter gobbins
The Good Lord protects the simple-minded

Tha'rt clever but tha'll dee
You may be more intelligent than I am, but you will
still die anyway

He's getten moor in is yed than nits
He has more in his head than nits
He is very clever

He'd gi thi his arse an shit through his ribs
He is a most generous person

It weynt eight grass
It won't eat grass
A rather low reference to the female pudendum in
a period of separation from boyfriend or husband;
indicates the speaker thinks he has a chance of
'scoring'

Exclamations!!!!!!!

Nay belike!
(Surely you jest?)

Fairation!
(Let us have some fair play, please.)

Partly wot!
(Nearly.)

Clap 'owd!
(Hold tight!)

Gulladowdlad!
(Well done, sir!)

Weigh!
(Stop!)

Think on!
(Remember.)

Bidooin!
(Hurry up!)

Ah cawn't speyk!
(I stand amazed!)

Shittot!
(Great.)

Guwomwithibother!
(I don't believe you.)

Four cakes!
(An exasperated euphemism.)

Neh then!
(Depending on how it is said, this can mean "hello" or "beware".)

That licks cock-feight!
(Superb!)

It'll come to thee!
(You'll get paid back.)

Winkayltum!
(We have defeated them.)

What con yer do when yer clogs let watter in?
(An exclamation of resignation.)

Family Matters

Here is some healthy advice to outsiders who are tempted to meddle with family matters in Lancashire. *DON'T.*
Here are some phrases to keep amongst the family:-

They're lahk tribe uv Israel.
(They are a rather large family.)

Kick one – an' they aw faw deawn. (all fall down).
(They are very close-knit.)

We're related to 'em – their cat ran through our backyard.
(We are not all that closely related really.)

They fun eawt (found out) what wur causin' it.
(They are now taking precautions against having any more children.)

'Eez nobburra lad awom.
(He might be a big shot at the office, but at home he's a cipher.)

'Eez 'is feyther shitten.
(He is a perfect facsimile of his father.)

Nay – 'e favvers 'is mam.
(I disagree – he looks more like his mother.)

They 'ad a bite ut th' apple afore they bowt tree.
(They enjoyed very close relations before they married.)

It's nobbut cowd porridge waarmed up.
(Cold porridge warmed up – a renewal of old love as when a divorced couple re-marry.)

'Eez babbed 'er an' theyn 'a t' get wed.
(He has made her pregnant and they have had to marry.)

'Er'll clog again.
(She will marry again.) (of a widow).

They're livin' o'er t'brush.
They're livin' tally.
(They are cohabiting unmarried.)

'Eez gettent feet undert th' essole wi' t'widder next door.
(He seems to be getting on rather well with his widow neighbour.)

T' Wahf...

In Lancashire, the men prefer not to refer directly to their wives...especially in front of pub cronies or workmates. Instead, they will call them "t'dragon" (as opposed to "th' owd dragon" for the mother-in-law)..."t' bride" (if they are feeling charitable)...or even "th' owd 'andbrake" when their wives have put a stop to their social activities.

If the husband goes out in direct disobedience of his wife's wishes, this can lead to "a bad wom" (getting a bad home - ie. being in disfavour at home) or even "deaf'n'dumb meals" - prolonged silences at the dining-table for an indefinite period. This tactic is an effective method of coercing the husband to abide by his wife's demands - at least until the next time he decides to please himself what he does. This course of action usually results in the husband "getting his tap stopped", forcing him to lead a celibate existence until he repents.

Buying Clothes*

*BEIGHIN' CLOOERS

Anyerenny?
Have you got any?

Gollies
Galoshers

Nebbers
Peaked flat
caps

Dolly 'ats
Bowler hats

Cozzies
Bathing costumes

Cardies
Cardigans

Shoon
Shoes

Canal barges
Large shoes

Snotrags
Handkerchiefs

Brats
Aprons

Kecks
Knickers
Trousers

Britches
Trousers

Mufflers
White scarves

Sherts
Shirts

Ganzies
Jerseys

Jarmers
Pyjamas

The Weather

It favvers cowd eawt
It seems to be cold outside

It's fleein
It is most inclement

It's teeminorain
Heighvin deawn
Peltin deawn
Cukkin it deawn
Cummin deawn i' bukkitfuls
Peeindeawn
It is raining very hard

It's slutchy
It is muddy

Am frozzen
Brr – I'm really cold

Ahm sogginweet throo
My clothes are drenched

Owd Sol's eawt!
Hurray – the sun is shining!

Who's Not Who

Here are some strange-sounding Lanky names which refer not, as the traveller may think, to actual people – but to things...

JENNY GREENTEETH
A mythical boggart based on the green slime in brooks, supposed to drag down unsuspecting children to their doom.

WET NELLY.
A type of cake.

MARY ANN.
An effeminate man.

SWAGGERIN' DICK.
A type of toffee.

DOLLY TUB.
A large tub for washing clothes.

DOLLY BLUE.
An agent used for whitening clothes.

BILLY WINK.
A nursery name for the make-believe man who shuts children's eyes at bedtime. Thus, going to sleep is "getting some Billy Wink".

HARRY LONGLEGS.
The crane fly.

PEGGY WEGGIES.
A child's name for teeth.

RICK RACKS.
A pair of bones, struck together as a percussion instrument.

SOPHIE.
A sofa.

GREEN GILBERT.
Nose mucous.

Some southern misconceptions about Lancashire...

"It *always* rains in Manchester."
Wrong. This is a filthy falsehood put about by a Southerner who, on a visit to Manchester, caught a trout in his turnups in Albert Sqaure and was arrested for illegal fishing by a policeman with a bill and webbed feet.

"They spend fifty per cent of their time in the pub."
Wrong. This is a gross slur. The figure is nearer ninety per cent...

"They absolutely hate Southern people."
Wrong. We absolutely *love* Southerners - fried in batter, with a few chips...

"They do nothing but race their whippets all day long."
Wrong. We *used* to race whippets but we stopped doing it because they kept beating us.

"They eat their young and paint their faces blue."
Wrong. The blue faces are a manifestation of the extremities of the cold climate - and we only eat our young when there's an R in the month.

"Of course, my dear, they never ever bath..."
Wrong. We bath extremely regularly - once a year when we go to the seaside. How do you think *Blackpool* got its name?

"All Lancastrians wear clogs and shawls and flat hats all the time."
Wrong. We only wear them in bed.

"They constantly live on a diet of tripe."
Wrong. The only time we see tripe is when Southern football teams come to play us up North.

"And of course they are *totally* illiterate..."
Bolax!

Some Quaint Lanky Customs...

Spittin' on t' fire: a great source of amusement especially to old cocks in taprooms who compete to see who can put the fire out first. It makes a helluva mess of gasfires, though...

Dad's night out: traditionally a Friday...and a Saturday...and a Sunday...and a Monday etc.

Purrin' t' kettle on: Lancashire folk are always putting the kettle on. It helps if you have a flat head.

Noggin' a stockin': the practice of hiding the hole in the heel of a worn stocking underneath the foot by means of tugging at the toe end and tucking it under. It is very effective with woollen socks but stretches your suspenders to breaking point if you're wearing a pair of nylons.

Bottomin' th' eawse: bottoming the house. This means giving the house a thorough cleaning from top to bottom – *not* walking about without trousers.

Donkey-stonin' t' steps: whitening the doorstep and the surrounding flags by rubbing them with a "donkey stone". This practice is steadily going into a decline due to shortage of donkey stones caused by the intervention of the RSPCA on behalf of the donkeys. (Only joking – it's a sort of pumice.)

Chukkin' t' cap in: a method of ascertaining whether or not one is welcome in a house by opening the door and throwing one's cap in. If it stays inside it either means you are welcome; there's nobody in; or your cap has landed on the fire.

Standing a round in t' pub: the Lanky mon always insists on standing a round in the pub. In fact he'll stand around all day and let you pay for the ale!

Fancyin' pigeons: a disgusting habit carrying a penalty of six months for the first offence.

Useful Words and Phrases...
Plus odds'n'sods

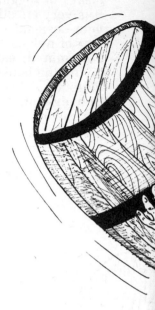

It's aw up-brew
It is all up hill

Awluvva ruck
All together – crowded

Varnyear
Nearly

Sex
Sacks

Lozz
Lie idly about

Slopstone
Sink

Mank
To act the fool

Gawm
To recognise, acknowledge

Chunner
Mutter, natter at someone

Ah cawnt win a kest
I can't win anything

Keck o'er
Topple over

Slurr
Slide

Bingo's loosin'
The bingo hall is emptying

Mee-maw
To make faces at

Chelp
Impertinence

Had up
Summonsed by the court

Booath on uz
The two of us

Grotch/Golly/Goz/Gob
Expectorate

Yonmon
Him

Turr-arse abeawt
Rush about

A reet nicker-gripper
A frightening situation

Muck er nettles
All or nothing

Wazzums
Worms

Up at crack o' sparrowfart
To rise early

Rootin' an tootin'
Being inquisitive

Duck muck
Mucus in eye from sleeping

O'erlied
Overslept

A midgy's widgy off
A bug's dick off
Very close

Wap one on
Put one on

Wur poo'd eawt
We are very busy

Ah've gorra lassoo . . .
I've got a girl who . . .

Backerts an forrerts
Backwards and forwards

Ahmet
Not an Indian name – it means 'I might'

Carryin' on/Nannyin'
Illicit love

Sprag up
To bolster up

W'ir squits!
We're equal!

It's a bus-rahd away
It is a fair distance

Pog
Steal

Spiggy
Spearmint

Owt abeawt owt abeawt!
Expression of disbelief

Ah seed it
I saw it

Farnitcher
Furniture

Tha never sez!
I don't believe it!

Is thi' clugs clent?
Are your clogs clean?

Grawl
To molest a young lady

Tissue-papper ears
Said of someone who hears what they're not supposed to hear

Ahlsitmieer
I will sit down here

Ah keep gooin wi't yed deawn
I struggle through life

Art cooertin?
Are you seeing a member of the opposite sex?

Tha'rt slow uz a godshorse
You are extremely tardy

They'n flit
The persons you seek have moved house

Pots fer rags
Silly

Farriners
Newcomers to a district

Ah'm fast!
I am stuck!

Frikky!
You are a scaredy-cat

Setdi
Saturday

Moggy
Mouse or tiny insect

Nowtyback
Naughty child

Th'owd mon
Said endearingly of a youngster

Th'owd stockin'-mender
The wife

Rucks/Ruckins
Slag heaps

Razzer
Reservoir

Thrutch
A beautiful all-purpose word meaning to strain or push

Bobby's winder
A hole in a stocking

Crabby/Crawpy/Jammy/Spawny
Lucky

Purler/Blahnder/Dormer/Belter!
Good one!

Ahm not coddin', it wur rotten good
I deceive you not, it was brilliant

Peg eawt/Dee
Die

Peg up
Lift up

It stunk mon's height
It smelled a great deal
(to the height of a man)

Ah wur cawed gooin' wom
I was supposed to be going home

Pow
Haircut

Pow-slap!
An old Lancashire custom whereby a person who
has just had a haircut is given a slap on the back of
the neck

Wick
Week/Alive

Sloppy daw-daw
Kiddies term for mud

Dost yarmi?
Can you hear me?

Stop gerrinagate
Please stop annoying me

Hawf-soaked
Slow-witted

It's a beltin' little tenter
It is a very good guard dog

Some Advice

And now a few words of "friendly" advice... tek heed, *or else...*

Save thi breath fer t' cool thi porridge.
Let thi meight (meat) stop thi meawth.
(Eat up and shut up.)

Throw thi muck wheer thi love lies.
(Take your litter home with you.)

Tak no notice on 'em – they talk as they worm.
(They converse through their bottoms.)

Don't pull t' pictures deawn – wur not flittin'.
(Father, *do* stop picking your nose!)

Shut thi' legs – there's a draught!
(Please keep your knees together, madam.)

Don't wait o' shoon (shoes) till clogs wain't come.
(Advice to a young woman who wants to marry "above" herself but might find herself left on the shelf.)

Keep it dark – it met (might) be a black puddin'.
(Nonsense phrase to emphasize that something you have been told, or found out, is in the strictest confidence.)

Spit it eawt – it met (might) spell it.
(Advice to a stutterer.)

Lap up.
(Wrap up warm – it's cold outside.)

Ball off an' bounce.
(Shove off!)

Keep thi' motty eawt, serry.
(Do not meddle in my affairs.)

Expletives*

*SWURR-WURDS

Ecky pecky thump! (very mild)

Skennin' eck! (tame)

By the stars! (innocuous)

By the crin! (permissible in polite company)

Ah'll go ter the foot of eawr sturrs! (traditional)

Ah'll go ter mi tay! (inoffensive)

Flamin' hanover!! (slightly stronger)

Owd mon!! (a reference to the devil?)

By the roastin mon!! (the devil again?)

Blood and sand!! (moderate)

Blood and stomach pills!! (rather forced)

By the jimmy nigger!! (discriminatory?)

Bluddy nora!!! (rather strong)

Jerr-usalem!!! (slightly profane – a vicar-shocker)

Buggamee!!! (very strong)

Hells bells of buggery!!!!! (use only under extreme provocation – and don't let your mother hear you)

Yanky goes Lanky

The buck stops here, me owd sugar butty! Far too many people these days talk like they've just stepped out of a cheap American B-movie. Battered into submissive acceptance by a plethora of television imports from the U.S.A. (and I don't mean the Uther Side of Accrington), we are swapping our mother tongue for an uncle tongue – Uncle Sam's to be precise.

It's got to stop. To help reverse the flow, here are some typical "yankifications" I have translated into good owd Lanky...

YANKY: Lay some skin on me...
LANKY: Pass the black puddin's.

YANKY: Keep on trucking.
LANKY: Don't give up your job at Pickfords.

YANKY: Right on.
LANKY: No foreplay (a typical Lanky Chauvinist Pig tactic).

YANKY: Rip-offs.
LANKY: Petty rolls (toilet paper).

YANKY: Hang loose.
LANKY: A bad case of Brewer's Droop.

YANKY: She's far out, man.
LANKY: 'Er's expectin' a babby.

YANKY: She's a real little mover.
LANKY: 'Er's always flittin'.

YANKY: Laid back.
LANKY: The fate of the recipient of a Wiggin butty. (a smack in the gob).

YANKY: He's an acid freak.
LANKY: He likes lots of vinegar on his tripe.

YANKY: A real cool chick.
LANKY: A deep-frozen turkey.

YANKY: Black is beautiful, man.
LANKY: Gi'me a black puddin' ony day, serry.

YANKY: Stay cool.
LANKY: Don't pay yer gas bill.

YANKY: Cop out.
LANKY: In Lancashire, this question is traditionally asked of anglers after a day's fishing.

YANKY: What's your bag, man?
LANKY: What does the mother-in-law do for a living?

Going, Going – Gone?

It is a sad thing when a good word dies. Here are some apt and colourful Lanky words which although dead or dying, seem much more expressive than their tame modern counterparts. Perhaps we could give them the kiss of life?

Good lorjus days.
Good lord Jesus
– what days.

Yonderly.
An almost poetic adjective meaning absent-minded or not quite "with it".

Warch.
Ache.

Arsey versey.
Head over heels.

Hiddlance.
In secret.

Powler.
To ramble about, drinking.

Addle.
Earn.

Ninny 'ommer.
Fool

Jannock.
Honest and good.

Rift.
Belch.

Scarrick.
A tiny piece of something.

Gobslotch.
A glutton.

Day skrike.
Day break.

Edge o' dark.
Twilight.

Old Lancashire Toast

Meyt (food) when we're hungry
Drink when we're dry,
Brass when we're short on it
An' Heaven when we die!

Eee It's a Lowf Innit!

Take care when riding a bicycle through the streets of Lancashire. The following shouts can be heard frequently coming from children:

Whooz deed?
Who has died?
Said to a person with trouser-leg
bottoms above their ankles,
i.e. half mast

Gerroff an' milk it!
Get off and milk it!

Eigh – dust know thi back wheel's follerin' thi' frunt un?
Do you realise your back wheel is following your front one?

Q: What con ah haft eight mam?
What can I eat, mother?
A: Three run jumps up buttery dooer – an when tha gets theer, slurr deawn
Three running jumps up the pantry door – and when you get there, slide down

Q: What's that tha'rt making?
What are you making?
A: Layholes fer meddlers an' crutches fer lame ducks
Nonsense phrase intended to rebuff stupid question

Tha'll bi lahk Morty's Donkey
This is said to be a person who refuses to eat his food, it refers to an apocryphal tale about a certain man named Mort who had just got his donkey used to living without food when it died

Th'art up early – ast peedibed?
Said to an early riser, it insinuates that the person has risen for reasons other than the desire to be up early

Crows'll mess on yer
Said of someone who has no new clothes for Easter – it arises out of the supersitition that the crows single out such unfortunate people and 'spot' them

83

Heigh thee – cum here!
And when the dupe all unsuspectingly returns, the joker quips merrily:
Heaw far wutta bin if theaw hadn't come back?
How far would you have been if you hadn't come back? To which the dupe replies, if he is of razor-sharp mentality:
Twice length uv a foo' (fool). **Lie deawn while ah measure thi'**
The biter bit!

Q: **Who is it? Who's theer?**
A: **Icky – fire bobby!**
   A mythical Lancashire personality

Q: **Is it rainin'?**
   To someone who is drenched
A: **No, ah've just pooered a bukkit o' waiter o'er mi yed.**
   No – I've just poured a bucket of water over my head

Q: **Warrat gawpin' at?**
   What are you looking at?
A: **Ah dunno – label's dropped off.**
Q: **Ast getton thi eenfull?**
   Have you got your eye full?
A: **Aye**
A: **Well turn reawnd and get t'other full**

Q: **Dust wanna picture?**
A: (Either) **No ta – ah don't collect 'orrer pictures**
   (Or) **Aye – it'll do fer frikkenin'** (frightening) **cats off petty waw** (lavatory wall)

Gerreawt o't leet – tha weren't made i' St Helens.
Get out of the light – you were not made in St Helens

Said to someone obstructing a person's view, it refers to the glass that St Helens is famous for manufacturing

Bi sharp theer an back, an if tha faws, don't stop gerrup
Be quick there and back, and if you fall, don't stop to get up.
Think about it . . .

Skoobells gone
The schoolbell has sounded
A: Whooz tan it?!
Who's taken it?
This witty response loses something in the translation.

UNSUSPECTING TRAVELLER: I say there, you chappy – have you got a match?
WITTY LANKY MON: Aye – thy face an my arse

Tha'rt gooin't meet thiself cummin back
Slow down

Put thi' torch eawt – it's meltin mi ice-lolly!
Facetious cry to usherette in cinema

Bits'n'Bobs . . .

(some useful words and phrases to help you
on your way)

It wur a reet knacker-wratcher.
(It was rather hard work.)

Babby-werk. (baby-work)
(A childish action by a grown-up.)

Parish lantern.
(The full moon.)

Parish candles.
(Stars.)

Axum back.
(Ask them back.)

Beggar uv it wur . . .
(The irony of it was . . .)

A stonkin' greight lorronem.
(A great many of them.)

Mangy.
(Ill-tempered.)

Mi eyes're swoppin' corners.
(I am growing extremely tired.)

Pisspoor.
(Very poor. A criticism, not a financial statement.)

Meitherin'.
(Pestering, annoying.)

Witchert.
(Wet-shod: the state of having wet feet.)

It's aw baws (all balls).
(A reference to the game of snooker.)

Spon-new, or Sponny.
(Brand-new.)

Neet ullet.
(Night owl – used to describe person who stays out late at night.)

Incense.
(In Lancashire, "I couldn't incense him", means "I couldn't make him understand".)

Lugg.
(A knot in the hair.)

Bacon tree.
(Pig.)

Cryin' a notchel.
(Giving public notice – usually in local paper – that one party won't be responsible for debts of another.)

Car thi deawn.
(Please sit down.)

Showin' yer monkey.
(Acting up or becoming bad-tempered.)

Th'oon.
(The oven.)

Cow clap.
(Cow pat.)

Sindin' t'clooas.
(Rinsing clothes.)

If *Ah* cawn't catch thi mi *dog* will!
(Said when throwing an object at someone you are pursuing.)

Pissfartin'.
(Of little consequence.)

Hanch.
(To snap at - as a dog snapping with its teeth. The Hallowe'en game of biting at apples on strings is known as hanch-apple.)

Nast.
(Dirt. Filth. Or as used by a workman before changing into clean clothes - "I'm in me nast".)

Obstrockolus.
(A frequently-used Lancashire mispronunciation of obstreporous.)

Rammy.
(Food that smells off.)

Thrashers.
(Old slippers still in use.)

Rider-eawt.
(A brewery representative calling at pubs.)

Stotherin' drunk.
(Staggering drunk.)

Yorkshire Oyster.
(An egg.)

Peighlin' away.
(Hurrying. Also used of a sexual encounter as in "Ah wur peighlin' away when her husband walked in".)

Bant.
(String.)

Wi' leet on um.
(We came across them.)

Buzzert.
(Moth.)

Darkin'.
(To go spying on courting couples at night.)

Arrin' an' jarrin'.
(Arguing.)

Th'art a maulin' scone!
(You are a meddlesome so-and-so.)

Ah cud do wi' a dose o' brokken bottles.
(I'm constipated.)

Parrotin' on. Pappin' on.
(Talking excessively.)

Sooly.
(Dirty.)

A ponful.
(A lot.)

Deggin' can.
(Watering can.)

Back eend.
(Autumn.)

Thrayklin' wom. (Treacling home).
(To wend one's way home.)

Ah cud eight (eat) a scabby-yedded Chinamon.
Ah cud eight neb off me cap.
(I am extremely hungry.)

Cut.
(Canal.)

Tha shapes lahk a wooden 'orse.
(You are useless.)

Britches-arse steam.
(Very hard manual effort.)

Cheese'n'Tripe!
(A blasphemous euphemism.)

Tek thi face a-rattin'!
(Advice to ugly man...)

Funnyossities

You can expect to have the mickey taken out of you in Lancashire.

Watch out for the following...

Traveller: Excuse me, I wonder...
Lanky Mon: (interrupting) Tha'd wonder wuss (worse) if t' crows built in thi yed and took thi nose fer a nest egg...
Or, (slightly stronger version):
Lanky Mon: Tha'd wonder wuss if t' crows built up thi arse - tha'd wonder how they'd getten sticks across!

Traveller: Excuse me - have you got the correct time?
Lanky Woman: Aye - a quarter past mi garter an' hawf-road (halfway) up me leg.
Traveller: (bemused) Thanks very much.

A: I've just been thinking...
B: Oh aye - Ah wondered what that rattle were...

Child: Mam - Ah've nowt sit on...
Mam: Well shove thi thumb up thi arse and sit on thi' elbow...

Beware of this following prank which can only be used on New Year's Eve.
A: Where are you going?
B: Ah'm gooin t' look fer t' mon who 'as as many noses on 'is face as there are days in t' year.

After which person A is expecting to see a man with 365 noses on his face until it suddenly dawns on him that there's only *one* day left in the year. Ho Ho.

The traveller should also be wary when he sees a sign saying "For the blind", with a collecting box underneath it outside a grocer's shop. It has been known for the shopkeeper to wait until the collecting

90

box is full – then go out and buy himself a new blind for the shop-window.

Lanky Mon: Hey thee – what's a turd weigh?
Foolish Traveller: I haven't the faintest idea...
Lanky Mon: (*hardly able to contain his glee*) 'Ere's a penny – go an' weigh thiself!

If the traveller is wearing a cap, he should beware of the following prank...

Lanky Mon: Hey Ah say – let me see if there's a wee in thi cap....
And when the unwary traveller passes him the cap in all good faith, the Lanky mon whizzes it gleefully across the street shouting: "Wheeeee!"

A: I see (local fishmonger) has just been fined £50.
B: What for?
A: For showing his cod in t' shop winder...!

(A play on the word "cod" which could either mean the fish of that name, or what a codpiece covers.)

Picture a tiny man on a large horse in a parade...
Heckler: Oi – shortarse... why dussn't geroff and ger inside it?
Small Man: If its arse were as big as thy gob, I'd 'ave no trouble at all.

Traveller: But I thought...
Lanky Wit: Tha knows what thowt did – he followed a muck cart and thowt he were followin' a weddin'. Or, – he shittibed an' thowt he were on t' petty.

Cry to someone scratching their head...
"Turn 'em over an' gi' t' young 'uns a chance! (meaning give the young nits a chance to come on top.)

Person rushing up: Ah've come fer t' tell thi Ah can't come – an' if Ah come Ah can't stop...!

If in Lancashire you buy a meat and potato pie and there is more potato than meat, the bits of meat are whimsically called sheawters (shouters) because they are so far apart in the pie that they have to shout to one another in order to converse. Also known as a Hurray Pie – because every time you find a piece of meat you shout *"Hurray!"*

"Go an' see if yer outside – and if yer return while yer away, I'll keep yer 'ere till yer get back..."
(Einstein couldn't even work *that* one out.)

Irate Housewife: Beauty is only skin deep....
Husband: Then tha must've bin born insahd eawt.

All Together Now!

Lancashire words have a tendency to run all to-gether. This may confuse the unaccustomed ear but it does save time, that is unless you have to explain to the unaccustomed ear what it was you were saying in the first place.

Willy Eckerslike
He will not

Avennyonyerennyonyer?
Have any of you any on you?
(matches, money, etc.)

Weyntajust?Theeseeifadoant!
Oh won't I? You will see!

Wivgettentgutsleep
We have to go to sleep

Artshoorothat?
Are you positive?

Aberragerralorravum
I bet I get a lot of them

Azzyettenworrizgetten?
Has he eaten what he's got?

Weeaffertguffertbuzz
We must leave now – our bus is due

Yacht?
Is it too warm in here for you?

Astbinmenbinmam?
Have the refuse collectors called yet, mother?

93

The Great Moggy Controversy

1. Take one taproomful of mixed Lancastrians.
2. Add beer.
3. "Stir it" by shouting: "What's a moggy?"
4. Stand back and watch the mixture simmer.

The result will be a red-hot potato...and if all that seems a bit cockeyed, let me explain:

There is one word in Lancashire of nobbut five letters which at its mere mention has the power to set brother Lanky against brother Lanky and start a civil war throughout the county.

It is the one thing which has more power to divide the county than a whole cartload of planners and bureaucrats put together.

The word is (don't shout it!)

MOGGY!

You see, part of the county says a moggy is a cat...part says it is most definitely a mouse! And some even go so far as to say it's also creepy-crawly insects and nits.

In the companion volume to this book – *Lanky Spoken Here!* – I defined a moggy as being a mouse or tiny insect. That really put the cat among the moggies or the moggy among the pigeons (depending on which side of the moggy fence your sympathies lie).

Moggy battle standards were raised all round the county, resulting in strong letters to the press; hour-long phone-ins with Alec Greenhalgh (pro-cat) on Radio Manchester; a running battle in the *Manchester Evening News* between myself and writer Andrew Grimes; moggy cartoons in the papers; plus shoals of letters and learned scholars of the dialect joining in the general scrum.

The outcome of all which was this:-

It was agreed that in some parts of Lancashire – mainly the coalmining areas – a moggy is a mouse and in some parts it's a cat (though coming from the part of Lancashire where a moggy is a mouse, I know what it *really* is....)

So, if you want to start off a good old Lancashire barney, simply casually enquire: "What *is* a moggy...?" Then run like hell.

Some Moggy Expressions

Moonleet Moggy. (moonlight moggy) – a beautifully descriptive term for a loose woman...one who stays out late at night.

Moggy is also a nickname for a very small person.

Moggy muck – mouse droppings.

Moggy meight (mouse food) – cheese.

Moggy off! Lanky for "Go away!"

A Moggy-er or Moggy-catcher is a cat (but only in those parts of Lancashire where a moggy is a mouse).

Moggy-yed – an abusive call after someone with nits in their head.

Moggy Pie – is, believe it or not, a pie made out of baked mice and used as a cure for bedwetting.